IN SEARCH OF THE LOST GALAXY

A two act play

Written by Colin Fantham

ISBN: 978-1-917425-19-3

CHARACTERS

Old Man

Psychiatrist

Intruder

President of WGO

Grogan

Fedo

Samile

Hetta

Delgin

Habel

Patora

Jezra

Santon

Armed Guard #1

Armed Guard #2

Armed Guard #3

ACT ONE

SCENE ONE

Sad music.

Psychiatrist's office, sparsely furnished, situated in a plush tower block. Dimly lit. Large screen, upstage centre, depicting window of office showing tall futuristic buildings in distance. A storm is brewing and dark clouds are forming. Two leather armchairs, downstage centre, facing each other.

> *The female psychiatrist, early thirties, formally attired, holding a notepad and pen, stands by the window looking out. An old man, casually attired, slowly enters the room, stage left. The old man has a tired, defeated expression, as if life has lost its meaning.*

Music fades.

Psychiatrist I've been expecting you. [*Turns to Old Man and gestures for him to sit*] Please… take a seat.

> *The Old Man looks unsure of his surroundings.*

Old Man Thank you for seeing me.

> *The Old Man sits in the left armchair. The Psychiatrist sits opposite him.*

Psychiatrist Tell me, Mister… [*Looks briefly at her notepad but does not pursue it*] What brings you here?

The Old Man stares blankly ahead, as if in another world; his response comes painfully slowly as it does throughout their entire meeting. The Psychiatrist makes occasional notes in her notepad.

Old Man   I think I must be losing my mind.

Psychiatrist   And why do you think that is?

The Old Man considers at length.

Old Man   I seem to inhabit a world that is alien to me.

Psychiatrist   In what way?

Old Man   In dreams...

Psychiatrist   Dreams?

The Old Man nods.

Old Man   More like nightmares.

Psychiatrist   [*smiles*] We all dream. They're part of the human condition. Now and then we all experience images that may be... *disturbing.*

Old Man   Not like... *this.*

Psychiatrist   Sigmund Freud suggests that dreams represent our unconscious desires, our thoughts, wish fulfilments... fears. They're not a physical manifestation; more of an internal reflection of ourselves, perhaps.

Old Man   And you believe that?

Psychiatrist   Don't *you?*

Old Man   I don't know what to believe. None of it makes sense to me. But they

feel so real. My fear is that one day I'm going to fall asleep and then I'll

be lost in them...

Psychiatrist   That isn't going to happen.

Old Man   How can you be so sure?

The Psychiatrist ponders this question.

Psychiatrist   I'm here to help you.

Old Man   I think I may be beyond help.

Psychiatrist   Nobody is beyond help. That's why *I'm* here. That's why *you're* here.

The Old Man looks imploringly at Psychiatrist.

Old Man   How can I be sure that *you're* real? That any of *this* is real? For all I know

you could just be inside my head.

Psychiatrist   I assure you that I'm real. Think of me as your friend.

Old Man   Friend?

Psychiatrist   You can trust me.

Old Man   I don't have friends. I'm not sure I can trust anyone.

Psychiatrist   I'm not your enemy.

Old Man   No… [*embarrassed*] of course you're not. You must think me paranoid?

Psychiatrist You came here seeking help. That's the first step on the ladder to redemption.

Old Man Redemption?

Psychiatrist I can sense that you have deep-rooted anxiety, perhaps brought on by a feeling of… insecurity?

Old Man I'm not known for being insecure. Quite the opposite. But lately… it feels as though my life has lost its meaning. That I'm in the hands of… *others*.

Psychiatrist Others? In what way?

Old Man It's as though I'm part of some mad existence.

Psychiatrist We all feel vulnerable at times in our lives. Stress can be a powerfully negative force. It can be very destructive to our mental health. When one feels engulfed with-

The Old Man shakes his head.

Old Man [*irate*] You don't understand. [*Sighs deeply*] Perhaps you never will…

Long pause.

Psychiatrist [*gently*] Help me to understand…

The Old Man looks to the heavens.

Old Man I haven't slept in days… You see, I dread falling asleep. That's when they come to me. They seem real. [*Looks around him*] As real as it is now. There *was* a time… [*Looks lost*] But that was long ago, I think. Can you imagine what it's like to meet your younger self? [*The Psychiatrist looks at the Old Man briefly, and then makes copious notes in her notepad*] It's as though I've entered a world of unreality. A world I don't recognise. And yet… somehow, I accept it for what it is. [*Considers at length*] Perhaps it *is* real… [*Stands and walks to window, and looks out to the world below*] We're all like ants aren't we? Working feverishly. All for the greater good of the majority. We seem to have lost the ability to be ourselves: individuals with our own identity; our own thoughts, ambitions, likes and dislikes. Forever being told what to do and when to do it. Like lambs to the slaughter…

Psychiatrist   You have a very pessimistic view of the world.

The Old Man looks to the Psychiatrist, and smiles sadly.

Old Man   I would seem to be a lost cause? Perhaps I should leave?

The Psychiatrist gestures the Old Man back to his seat.

Psychiatrist   We're making progress. Stay. Please. Your case is… *interesting.*

The Old Man slowly returns to his seat.

Old Man   What is your prognosis? Am I a madman?

The Psychiatrist consults her notes, and then addresses the Old Man.

Psychiatrist   You appear to have suffered a psychotic episode, perhaps triggered by emotional trauma. If we can determine the root cause of the trauma, we may be able to reduce the symptoms that show themselves during your sleep pattern. [*Long pause*] Before we review the nature of your… *dreams,* we need to identify precisely what concerns you may have… that have had such a detrimental effect on your mental well-being. Tell me about yourself. Are you retired?

Old Man   Because I'm old?

The Psychiatrist shrugs slightly.

Psychiatrist   Partly.

Old Man   I'm a writer. We never retire. [*Solemn*] At least not until that final chapter…

The Psychiatrist looks to the Old Man, with concern in her eyes.

Psychiatrist   And do you think you're close to that final chapter?

Old Man   I try not to think about it.

Long pause.

Psychiatrist   What do you write about?

Old Man   My stories are set in the future. At least, my interpretation of it.

Psychiatrist   And do you find that a fulfilling occupation?

Old Man   I used to.

Psychiatrist   Does your own future concern you?

The Old Man looks sad.

Old Man   As I said before, I try not to think about it.

Long pause.

Psychiatrist   Is your legacy important to you?

The Old Man smiles, but his eyes are empty.

Old Man   You're quite the Jiminy Cricket, aren't you?

Psychiatrist   Who?

Old Man   My conscience.

Psychiatrist   Oh…

Old Man   I want my work to be remembered.

Awkward pause.

Psychiatrist   Do you live a lonely life?

Old Man   All writers lead lonely lives. One becomes accustomed to one's own company. It's a solitary existence, I suppose, perhaps even… *abnormal*, but you can't be creative when surrounded by people. Too much of a distraction. It's the nature of the beast.

Psychiatrist   Your work must mean a great deal to you?

Old Man   It means everything to me. For good or bad.

Psychiatrist   Tell me about the bad.

Long pause.

Old Man   Literally being lost for words.

Psychiatrist   Writer's block?

The Old Man nods.

Old Man   It's the curse of the writer. Not being able to fill a blank page with words that have some meaning.

Psychiatrist   That must be very frustrating for you?

Old Man   Of course. It's my life blood. Without words *I* have no meaning. No… sense of purpose.

Psychiatrist   A lost soul?

The Old Man looks sad.

Old Man   A fitting analogy.

Psychiatrist   And how does that make you feel?

Old Man   How do you *think* it makes me feel?

Psychiatrist   You tell *me*.

Long pause.

Old Man   Redundant.

Psychiatrist   Redundant? In what way?

Old Man   No use to anyone. Least of all myself.

Long pause.

Psychiatrist   Tell me about your dreams.

Old Man   I wouldn't know where to start.

Psychiatrist   Take me back to the beginning. What was the first that you remember?

Lights fade.

SCENE TWO

Suspenseful background music.

A spacious modern open lounge smartly decorated. A tall staircase stage left. It is late at night. Large screen, upstage centre, depicting horizontal blinds, through which moonlight casts its pale glow within the room.

> *A young man, dressed in black, and using a small torch to see, can just be seen rifling through drawers, stage right; he accidentally knocks over an ornament, which makes a noise. An old man, wearing a dressing gown over silk pyjamas, seen slowly descending the staircase; he has a gun in his hand, and points it at the Intruder. Their voices, as in all dream sequences, resonate in a dream-like quality.*

Music fades.

Old Man   Whatever you're doing stop it immediately. I have a weapon, and I'm quite prepared to use it.

Intruder   Don't do anything stupid, old man. It's not what you think.

Old Man   I may be old… and perhaps decrepit… but I'm still perfectly able to pull this trigger if need be. You are hardly in a position to negotiate.

Intruder   That looks like an antique. It would probably blow your hand off if you pulled that trigger.

The Old Man is now at the bottom of the staircase and is facing the Intruder, across the room.

Old Man   That's very ageist of you. You shouldn't presume that because something, or some*one*, is of a certain age it is no longer of any value. A fine wine matures with age, as do I… [*to himself*] albeit with lumbago and an enlarged prostate.

Pause.

Intruder   [*to himself*] Not much for me to look forward to.

Old Man   Hmm? This is my family home. How did you get in?

Intruder   You left the back window unlocked.

Old Man   That was very careless of me.

Intruder   You're a creature of habit.

Old Man   And how would you know that?

Intruder   Let's just say I know you as well as I know myself.

Old Man   Are we acquainted with one another?

The Old Man switches on side wall lights, which cast a dull light throughout the perimeter of the room.

Intruder   More than you could possibly know.

Old Man   You look familiar to me, but I'm told that my memory isn't what it was. I'm hoping it's a temporary malaise.

Intruder   [*to himself*] I wouldn't hold my breath.

Old Man   Hmm? I shall call the police.

Intruder   Why?

Old Man   *Why?* Because you have been caught rummaging through drawers, obviously looking for valuables. Probably to support a nasty drug habit, I wouldn't wonder.

Intruder   I was looking for something… but not valuables.

Old Man   You'll be able to tell your unlikely story to the police.

The Old Man is about to pick up the telephone.

Intruder   I wouldn't do that if I were you. [*Laughs sardonically to himself*] The irony…

Old Man   I'm perfectly at liberty to shoot you if need be. Your demise would not affect me one way or the other. I have seen death at first hand many times during the last war.

The Intruder looks puzzled.

Intruder   What war?

Old Man   Hmm?

Intruder   You said you were in the last war.

Old Man   Ah… the ignorance of youth. I was perhaps a few years older than you when I received my call-up papers.

The Intruder looks shocked.

Intruder   Jesus.

Old Man   I enlisted as a drone attack operator. A very effective one at that. [*With pathos*] I've had to live with the consequences of my actions ever since. [*Long pause*] Didn't they teach you about the Great Conflict of seventy-five? Perhaps the obliteration of twenty cities throughout the world didn't merit a mention in your history lessons at school?

The Intruder looks directly at the Old Man.

Intruder   I went to Finburn College.

Old Man   Finburns? [*The Old Man considers at length*] I believe that's the same school that I attended… but it's been closed for over forty years. How is that possible?

Intruder   The headmaster was Sir Alfred Pinkhampton.

Old Man   [*shakes head*] Pinkhampton was an old man when *I* was at Finburns. Who are you exactly?

Intruder   I'm someone from your past. [*Sighs*] I've already said too much.

Old Man   You haven't said enough. I presume you have read my autobiography and are trying to play tricks with my mind. You should know that I am made of sterner stuff.

Intruder   I only know what I know from my own past. It's my future that concerns

me… your past.

Old Man   That is absurd. You can't change the past. Unless… you've come from the

future?

Intruder   *My* future isn't the past – it's the future.

The Old Man contemplates the young man's statement at length.

Old Man   If your future is *my* past then what am *I* doing here?

Intruder   In the past, *your* future doesn't exist.

Long pause.

Old Man   If the past has passed, we are living in the future.

Intruder   We live in the present. The future will never be the past.

Uncertain pause.

Old Man   I suddenly feel quite weary. [*Pause*] If you're saying what I think you're

saying, the World Governing Order outlawed improper use of transtemporal

displacement years ago.

Intruder   There were rogue elements within the WGO. You worked for them in your

youth.

The Old Man smiles knowingly.

Old Man   I think I would have remembered.

Intruder   Memories are supressed once you leave. You say that you have loss of mental capacity?

Old Man   There are moments in my past that I am unable to recall. It has been put to me that I am not as lucid as I once was. But I simply put that down to the ageing process.

Intruder   Your memory was wiped clean. You can never recall your time within the WGO. Standard practice. When I return… if I'm able… the same will happen to me… *you…*

Old Man   I'm not sure I believe a word of what you say. It's too… fantastical. You're playing mind games with me to protect your own skin. You're simply a burglar come to relieve me of my valuables.

The Old Man raises gun and points it directly at the Intruder's head.

Intruder   If you kill me, you'll be killing yourself. Your body will simply evaporate into the ether, as though you never existed… As though *we* never existed.

Old Man   You seem very sure of yourself. I am on the brink of extinction anyway. I have much less to lose than you.

Intruder   Please… don't. I'm not your enemy. Far from it…

The Old Man reluctantly lowers the gun, but holds it in readiness.

Old Man   I'm beginning to think that you are simply a warped part of my imagination. An illusion. All writers have the capacity to concoct a scenario of one sort or another. My mind must be playing tricks with me again.

Intruder   You're a writer?

The Old Man motions to the bookcase behind the intruder.

Old Man   There are twenty-three books on the bookcase over there with my name on. So… [*bows slightly*] guilty as charged.

The Intruder turns to the bookcase; each book has various titles but not the author's name.

Intruder   May I?

Old Man   [*sighs*] Why not?

The Intruder picks up a book, and browses through it.

Intruder   [*to himself*] At least that's *some*thing to be proud of.

Old Man   Hmm?

Intruder   Are all your books of this genre?

Old Man   [*nods*] They are all based on my interpretation of the future.

Intruder   Interesting…

Old Man   Oh? Why interesting?

Thoughtful pause.

Intruder   I wrote my first story when I was in my teens. You might remember it?

The Intruder returns the book to the bookcase.

Old Man   I don't see why I should.

Intruder   It was called The Lost Galaxy.

The Old Man looks visibly moved. Long pause.

Old Man   Good god... I'd forgotten all about that story. It must have been over fifty years ago.

Intruder   Less than ten for me.

Old Man   I still have it tucked away in a drawer somewhere.

Intruder   It must have meant something to you. Your first novel.

Old Man   I never let anyone else read it. Too embarrassed. Too… humble. It was very rough around the edges, you see.

Intruder   And yet you've kept it all these years.

Old Man   [*nods*] Gradually the stories improved. It was a passion of mine. Writing. I published my first novel after the war had finally ended. It kept me from losing my mind… and my spirit.

Intruder   It must have been a difficult time for you?

Long pause.

Old Man   Have *you* ever killed anyone?

The Intruder looks intently at the Old Man and shakes his head.

Intruder   [*quietly*] No… At least not yet…

Old Man   I haven't discussed it with anyone for over fifty years. You turn up and I'm giving you my life story. Strange… Why are you really here?

Intruder   To make sense of my life. Call it curiosity.

Old Man   And what have you found so far?

The Intruder looks to the Old Man with pathos in his eyes.

Intruder   From what you've told me I survived a global war, and became a competent writer. Quite a heady mix…

Old Man   You take the rough with the smooth. It's one lesson that I've learned in my long life.

Intruder   And yet it still troubles you?

Old Man   Actions have consequences.

Intruder   Such as?

The Old Man looks at the intruder with the pain of recollection etched in his eyes.

Old Man   Guilt.

Intruder   Guilt?

Old Man   Like a bad dream. It's tormented me for years. And always in the middle of the night. Without fail. It's taken me years to be able to live with it. To be able to write my stories. I suppose it's my one salvation. A way out of the darkness. Writing.

Intruder   An escape?

The Old Man nods.

Old Man   It's sustained me in my hour of need.

Long pause.

Intruder   You can trust me. Put the weapon down.

The Old Man considers at length.

Old Man   Against my better judgement I *do* feel a strange affinity with you. But until I am convinced that you are not a threat to my well-being, I will keep this weapon close at hand, if it's all the same to you.

The Old Man puts the gun in the pocket of his dressing gown.

Intruder   Suit yourself. [*Looks around the room*] It's a big house.

Old Man   I've lived here most of my life.

Intruder   Don't you share it with anyone?

Old Man   I prefer my own company. I've always been a loner. Comfortable in my own skin, I suppose.

Intruder   Don't you get lonely?

Old Man   On occasion.

Intruder   Sad. I always hoped I would have shared my life with another human being. Don't you have regrets?

Poignant pause.

Old Man   Of course. One learns to live with them. I suppose there are worse things in life.

Intruder   Like what?

The Old Man looks sad.

Old Man   How can I be sure you are who you say you are?

Intruder   Trust me. I am.

Old Man   Trust you? You are very persuasive, but for all I know you've come to rob me. Or worse…

Intruder   Stubborn as a mule.

Old Man   Put yourself in my position.

Intruder   I have no choice.

Old Man   [*getting angry*] You invade my space, and expect me to accept a story that is so ludicrous that-

Intruder   [*loudly*] You must use your judgement, old man.

Old Man   Easy for you to say. Words are cheap.

Intruder   For once in your life be REASONABLE.

Old Man   Reasonable? [*Walks towards telephone*] I'm calling the police. This charade has gone on for far too long.

Intruder   You need proof?

The Old Man picks up telephone receiver.

Old Man   Of COURSE I need proof.

The Intruder rolls up his left sleeve.

Intruder   I have a tattoo. [*Shows the Old Man a distinctive mark on his forearm*] Here.

The Old Man looks at the Intruder's forearm; he slowly replaces the receiver to its cradle, and walks to the intruder, and inspects tattoo.

Old Man   Good god.

The Old Man rolls his own left sleeve up, and compares the two tattoos.

Intruder   If that doesn't convince you, then…

The Old Man backs away from the intruder, as if in fright, and turns away.

Old Man   Why are you here?

Intruder   I *told* you… Curiosity. Perhaps to see if I was still alive and kicking.

Old Man   And now that you know?

Intruder   I know what I must do when I return.

Old Man   Which is?

Long pause.

Intruder   The right thing…

The Intruder looks downcast.

Old Man   Will I see you again?

Intruder   In time… Yes.

Long pause.

Old Man   It's so strange… but when I first saw you, a part of me, somewhere

deep inside, somehow knew, but the concept of it was too sublime; too

intense. [*The light on the Intruder begins to fade*] I'd begun to doubt that

I was *ever* young. Time seems to have gone by so quickly, and yet there

were days… [*Now in deep thought*] In the blink of an eye, as if by some

sleight of hand, I became this disillusioned Old Man that you see before

you now, forever lost in confusion with dark thoughts that haunt me still.

[*The Intruder is now nowhere to be seen*] I'd forgotten what it was to be

young; who I was and what I felt at the time. Seeing you has reminded

me that I really did exist. That that part of my life was real and not just

a part of some grand elaborate scheme.

*The Old Man looks for the Intruder, and realises that he is alone once
again; sadness is etched deep within his eyes.*

Suspenseful background music.

Lights fade.

Music fades.

SCENE THREE

Psychiatrist's office.

The Psychiatrist consults her notes.

Psychiatrist   The intruder was your former self?

Old Man   Without question.

Psychiatrist   How can you be so sure?

| **Old Man** | I *told* you. We shared the same tattoo in exactly the same place. |

The Psychiatrist makes brief note.

| **Psychiatrist** | And how did that make you feel? |

| **Old Man** | It felt good… at least until he was no longer there. |

| **Psychiatrist** | And when he was no longer there? How did *that* make you feel? |

The Old Man looks disconsolate.

| **Old Man** | Lost. |

Long pause.

| **Psychiatrist** | Do you remember much about your youth? |

| **Old Man** | Some of it. Lately there are a lot of blank pages. |

| **Psychiatrist** | That's an interesting turn of phrase… |

The Old Man seems disengaged; as if he was trying to remember something from his past.

| **Old Man** | Hmm? |

The Psychiatrist makes notes.

| **Psychiatrist** | You mentioned transtemporal displacement – what *is* that? |

| **Old Man** | Travelling in time. |

| **Psychiatrist** | Do you think that's possible? |

The Old Man looks at the Psychiatrist with incredulity.

Old Man   *Any*thing is possible. They said that humankind would never be able to fly… Now the sky is stuffed full with flying machines.

Psychiatrist   Do you still have feelings of guilt?

The Old Man looks sad.

Old Man   Yes.

Psychiatrist   You said your younger self worked for the World Governing Order?

Old Man   Apparently so.

Psychiatrist   And that memories are wiped clean upon leaving?

Old Man   What about it?

Psychiatrist   Do you feel that you have been part of some grand experimental scheme in your youth?

The Old Man looks agitated.

Old Man   That thought *had* crossed my mind.

The Psychiatrist consults her notes.

Psychiatrist   What was it that your younger self was looking for?

Old Man   I… I'm not sure.

Psychiatrist   Perhaps your first novel?

Old Man   Hmm?

Psychiatrist   The Lost Galaxy?

Old Man   My first full story.

Psychiatrist   Do you still have it?

Old Man   I haven't been able to find it. Perhaps it's lost forever.

Psychiatrist   Does that concern you?

Old Man   It was a part of me...

                   Long pause.

Psychiatrist   Tell me about your next dream…

Lights fade.

SCENE FOUR

Suspenseful background music.

Darkness. Slowly the large screen, upstage centre, shows in bold letters: WORLD
GOVERNING ORDER; beneath this is the decree: FOR THE GREATER GOOD OF THE
MAJORITY.

> *A man of obvious authority (50s) stands behind a lectern on a raised platform*
>
> *before the screen; he wears a dark military-style uniform. The man*
>
> *occasionally looks left to right, and vice versa, as he slowly speaks.*

President   Citizens of Mendetia… As your President of the World Governing Order, it

                   is incumbent upon me to inform you that the threat of instability, by those

                   seeking to subjugate us through their own warped political ideals… is real.

                   Murmurs of disapproval from a vast unseen crowd.

                   It has come to our attention that there are rogue elements amongst us: dark

26

forces who have abused their positions of authority; their reckless actions threaten the very nature of our continuance in this precarious world. They must be contained for the greater good of the majority.

The crowd displays its approval..

As written within our great and noble constitution, it is a punishable offence to violate the articles solemnly decreed therein, on your behalf, by the board of the World Governing Order.

Cheers from the crowd.

Those amongst us who are not fit for purpose shall be classed as Undesirables, and as such will be detained… and ultimately removed.

Applause and cheers.

Our place in this unsettled world has never been more fundamentally at risk. The ravages of devastation, created by the historical foolishness of mankind, has reduced the capacity of land fit for habitation. Food supplies remain woefully inadequate. Millions of our people are at risk of capitulation to the enemies of hunger and despair. Many thousands have already succumbed to their inevitable demise. Citizens… we must remain vigilant and obedient to the path that we have chosen.

Chants of "Mendetia" are heard amongst the crowd.

The resettlement programme, to galaxies other than our own, remains a priority, despite enormous burdens upon limited resources. We must continue along this path to ensure the prosperity of our children and future generations to come.

Loud applause.

Citizens… I remind you all that the World Governing Order was established to ensure the survival of our species; to navigate the perils that have been thrust upon us through ignorance and malevolent influence.

Cheers of approval.

It is essential that we are of one mind; that our ultimate destiny is not to be denied. We must prevent those that would stand in the way of our chosen path. Through discipline and fortitude, we *will* prevail.

Ecstatic approval by the crowd.

Those who fail to comply with the World Governing Order will be deemed traitors to the cause… They will NOT be tolerated… For the greater good of the majority.

The crowd erupts in cheers of "Long live Mendetia".

Lights fade.

Music fades.

SCENE FIVE

Psychiatrist's office.

The Psychiatrist consults her notes.

Psychiatrist   Let's discuss your dream. Perhaps we can make some sense of it.

Old Man   I'm not sure it makes *any* sense. It's just a madness.

Psychiatrist   Everything will make sense… Eventually.

Old Man   How can you be so sure?

Long pause.

Psychiatrist   The man who gave the address… You said he was the President of the World Governing Order?

Old Man   Apparently so.

The Psychiatrist looks intently at the Old Man.

Psychiatrist   Do you feel in life that you have to conform to an applied set of rules?

Old Man   Don't we *all*?

Psychiatrist   Why do you think that is?

The Old Man thinks long and hard.

Old Man   If you don't, you're seen as an outsider… You may as well be from another planet… Alienated.

Psychiatrist   I see…

Old Man   *Do* you?

Long pause.

Psychiatrist   You mentioned the address was to the citizens of Mendetia?

Old Man   What of it?

Psychiatrist   It's just that I've never heard of such a place.

The Old Man looks to the Psychiatrist. A sadness is in his eyes.

Old Man   You think I *have*?

The Psychiatrist considers at length.

Psychiatrist   Perhaps…

The Old Man feels agitated.

Old Man   I *told* you. I have no control over these… *dreams*.

Psychiatrist   Subconsciously there are meanings to all of our dreams. We just have to

find them.

Old Man   It's a needle in a very large haystack.

Psychiatrist   Nevertheless…

Old Man   The eternal optimist.

Psychiatrist   We're making progress…

Old Man   I'm not so sure.

The Psychiatrist consults her notes.

Psychiatrist   You said the President used the term: Undesirables.

The Old Man nods.

Old Man   Not fit for purpose.

Psychiatrist   Do you think that *you* are not fit for purpose?

Old Man   Lately I feel as though my life has no meaning.

Psychiatrist   In what way?

The Old Man looks briefly to the heavens as if seeking an answer.

Old Man   I no longer feel part of the human race.

Long pause.

Psychiatrist   Tell me about your next dream...

Lights fade.

SCENE SIX

Suspenseful background music.

A dark, dank, prison cell. Large screen, upstage centre, depicting barred window on high. Three figures are seen hanging from gallows in the distance, silhouetted against the moonlit sky. Tall, sturdy wooden door, stage left. Four long wooden benches positioned in a semicircle facing out, centre stage. The sound of water dripping on to the stone floor can occasionally be heard. Four prisoners, dressed in solemn prison uniforms, occupy this dismal enclosure.

> *Fedo (male early 20s) paces slowly about the prison; Hetta (aged female) lies on one of the central benches – she has a woollen blanket over her, and is clearly unwell; Grogan (male mid-40s) sits on bench stage left; Samile (female mid-40s) sits on bench stage right. Grogan looks to Fedo with irritation.*

Music fades.

Grogan   Must you keep pacing up and down, Fedo?

Fedo   What's it to you what I do?

Samile   Grogan's right. Save your energy.

Fedo   Save it for what? My execution?

Grogan   For your trial.

Fedo   I'm a thief. An Undesirable… just like all of *you*. Any excuse for them
to reduce the bloated population.

Samile   You're young. Perhaps that will work in your favour?

Fedo looks dispirited.

Fedo   The President made it clear that *all* Undesirables are surplus to requirement.
We don't stand a chance.

Hetta stirs.

Hetta   [*feebly*] Samile.

Samile rises and attends to Hetta.

Samile   I'm here.

Samile holds Hetta's hand.

Hetta   So thirsty...

*Samile goes to wooden bucket which has water in it, and fills a ladle; she
then returns to Hetta, who is now sat up, and gently feeds her the water.*

Grogan   Be thankful *you're* not old, Fedo.

Fedo   Thankful? At least Hetta has lived a life. I'm young. I'm not ready to die.

Grogan   No-one wants to die. It's just the way of this world.

Samile returns the ladle, and then sits beside Hetta.

Samile   Perhaps they'll find *another* world? A world fit for life?

Grogan   They've gone to countless galaxies. Perhaps there *is* no other world?

Fedo   What difference does it make to us? Our fate is already sealed.

Samile feels Hetta's forehead.

Samile   She has a temperature.

Grogan   They treat us like vermin. It's no sin to be old… at least it shouldn't be.

Fedo looks to the window.

Fedo   There should be a revolution. People should take to the streets. Fight for their rights. Instead, they're like sheep. Doing the bidding for the Order. As if they had no other choice.

Samile   The people are scared.

Hetta   [*wearily*] They have every right to be. It's history repeating itself.

Poignant pause.

Grogan   It shouldn't have to be this way. [*Grogan puts blanket about his shoulders*] They put me in here simply because I disagreed with the Order's doctrine, and made it known to others. The system is corrupt.

Fedo   You may as well have signed your own death warrant.

Grogan   Whatever happened to free speech?

Fedo   That's for other worlds. Not ours.

Grogan   We live in a world that controls the individual. If you have your own view they see you as: *Undesirable*. There has to be a different way. One that allows people the freedom to speak their mind. A better way of living.

Fedo   It's too late for us. Our fate is sealed. Look out of the window. That is our destiny. There is no salvation to be had.

Long pause. Samile walks back to her bench and sits.

Samile   How long will they keep us in this hell hole?

Hetta   Our time will come soon enough.

Samile   [*to Hetta*] Aren't you afraid?

Hetta   Death comes to us all… sooner or later.

Deathly hush.

Samile   I miss my boy so much.

Grogan   What happened to him?

Samile   He was taken from me. When I was arrested.

Grogan   I'm sorry.

Samile   He will be thirteen soon. I would give anything just to put my arms around him once more, and tell him that I love him.

Samile embraces herself for comfort.

Hetta   I'm sure he knows, Samile. You have a good heart.

Fedo   It seems so unfair... Why did they arrest you?

Samile in deep contemplation.

Samile   I killed my husband.

The others look to Samile in shock. Long pause.

Grogan   You must have had good reason.

Samile looks to the others, defensively.

Samile   I was in an abusive marriage. Octor was a cruel man. I was defending myself as well as my boy. [*Looks blankly ahead*] He had such hate in his eyes. I had no other choice. It was either him or us as God is my witness.

Hetta   God will forgive you, Samile.

Samile   I can barely forgive my*self*. But I would do it again. To protect my son. If this is to be my fate… then so be it.

Fedo   [*irritated*] God... Where was *He* when we needed him?

Hetta   He is inside all of us.

Fedo   [*dismissively*] He's not inside *me*.

Hetta sleeps.

Grogan   [*to Fedo*] What made you steal?

Samile   I'm sure Fedo had his reasons.

Fedo   My family are poor. We needed the money. We barely had enough to put bread on the table. Because food is scarce, the cost is so high. I had no choice. It was steal or starve.

Grogan   It's no sin to be poor, Fedo.

Fedo looks remorseful.

Fedo   I could have stopped. It became routine. [*Looks to others*] I could have stopped… Instead, I brought shame and dishonour to my family. [*Looks downcast*] Perhaps the Devil is inside me?

Grogan   It's the system. It's not fair. How can anyone follow the rules when it is so unjust? The Order has no conscience.

Samile   The Order has no soul…

Long pause.

Grogan   Perhaps… one day… the people will see the Order for what it is: a government that seeks to serve only those at the highest level, and disregards the rest of us. We are being sacrificed for the benefit of the privileged few. [*Samile gets up, walks to where Hetta is lying, and pulls the blanket up over her for warmth. She feels Hetta's forehead*] One day the people will remember us and change the world; create a new Order that is just and dignified; that treats all people fairly and with compassion. An Order that we can be proud of. Until that day… we will just be another statistic. Nameless faces lost in the mist of time…

Samile looks to the others; sadness is etched in her eyes.

Samile   [*solemnly*] Hetta is dead…

Suspenseful background music.

Lights fade.

Music fades.

SCENE SEVEN

Psychiatrist's office.

The Psychiatrist consults her notes.

Psychiatrist   Were any of the Undesirables known to you?

Old Man   No… except…

Psychiatrist   Yes?

The Old Man reflects long and hard.

Old Man   The woman that died somehow reminded me of somebody from my distant past. But I don't know who she was.

Psychiatrist   Your mother, perhaps?

The Old Man looks blankly ahead.

Old Man   Perhaps... but I can't be sure.

Psychiatrist   And when she died… in your dream… how did that make you feel?

Old Man   Sad. She didn't deserve to die in such a place.

Psychiatrist   Does the idea of death frighten you?

The Old Man shakes his head.

Old Man   Death comes to us all… sooner or later.

Long pause.

Psychiatrist   Do *you* feel like a prisoner?

Old Man   I feel… trapped. [*Sighs despairingly*] As though I am no longer in control.
So… yes. I suppose I do.

Psychiatrist   Interesting…

The Psychiatrist makes notes.

Old Man   Hmm?

Psychiatrist   We're making progress.

Old Man   I wish I had your faith.

Psychiatrist   I believe it all will begin to be clearer to you… In the end.

Old Man   The end... The final page.

Psychiatrist   Think of it as a new beginning.

Old Man   I'm think I'm too old for new beginnings.

The Psychiatrist consults her notes.

Psychiatrist   Do you think being old is a handicap?

The Old Man looks sad.

Old Man   Others seem to think so.

The Psychiatrist makes notes.

Psychiatrist   As though you don't belong anymore?

Old Man   That's very perceptive of you.

Psychiatrist   Are you worried that you will just be another statistic?

The old Man nods sadly.

Old Man   Forgotten…

Long pause.

Psychiatrist   Tell me about your next dream…

Lights fade.

SCENE EIGHT

Suspenseful background music.

Impressive meeting room. Long table centre stage with five high-backed chairs around it. Large screen showing elaborate emblem of World Governing Order.

Sat at the head of the table is the President. Seated around the table are five board members: Habel (male mid-20s), Santon (male early 40s), Jezra (female mid-20s), Patora (aged female), Delgin (aged male). Each of the five board members formally attired in black.

Music fades.

President   It has been brought to my attention, by Stellar Sixteen, that a planet has been detected in the outer reaches of the Herald Galaxy.

Delgin   The Herald Galaxy? I thought that was a lost cause?

The large screen now shows an image of a distant planet amongst a multitude of stars. Gradually the image begins to zoom in on the planet.

Habel   There are over a hundred billion stars in that region. It must have been like looking for a grain of sand.

They each glance at the screen.

Patora   A chance for resettlement...

Jezra   Is it a lifeless planet?

The President shakes his head.

President   Early indications are that advanced life forms inhabit this planet. Although vast in numbers, their technology is deemed to be greatly inferior to our own. [*Superciliously*] The entire planet, naturally, will need to be cleansed in order to accommodate resettlement by Mendetians.

Santon looks defeated.

Santon   War…

The President looks solemnly to Santon.

President   An inevitable consequence, Santon. One that cannot be avoided.

Habel   Can't terms be negotiated?

Jezra   It seems such an extreme measure.

The President maintains a stern expression.

President   We have five billion inhabitants on Mendetia. Our planet is dying at an unnerving rate. We must strike at the earliest opportunity. It is our only hope for long-term survival. [*Looks to Delgin*] Delgin…

Delgin   Mister President?

President   As Minister of Information, I want you to ensure that this news is not made common knowledge to the general populace. Anyone who leaks this information will suffer the consequences.

Delgin nods.

Delgin   Yes Mister President.

Patora   But surely the people deserve to know?

President   They will know when the time is right, Patora. Not before.

Santon   It seems wrong to eliminate an innocent life form. No matter the circumstances?

Jezra   Surely it goes against universal protocol?

The President looks agitated.

President   May I remind you all that we represent the World Governing Order. Our very existence is predicated on the survival of our species. The consequence of another life form's demise is irrelevant to the cause, as written in our great and noble Constitution. If you go against the rights of Mendetians, it is a violation as outlined Article Fourteen. I need to know that we are united in our quest. [*He looks at each in turn*] Habel?

The others each have a resigned look, knowing of the repercussions of going against the President; their replies are slow and solemn...

Habel   Agreed...

President   Santon?

Santon   Agreed...

President   Jezra?

Jezra   Agreed...

President   Patora?

Patora   Agreed...

President   Delgin?

Delgin   Agreed...

President   Then we are in accordance. [*Looks to Patora*] Patora...

Patora   Mister President?

President   Schedule a meeting with the Imperial War Cabinet. Firm and decisive action will need to be undertaken to ensure that the… *removal* of our adversaries, by our landing forces, is swift and complete.

Patora   Very well.

The President stands, looks briefly at the screen, and then turns to the others.

President   Think of it... the beginning of a new chapter. History will show that the leadership of the World Governing Order was strong and decisive; that I showed courage and conviction in eradicating our enemy and creating a new world. A world fit to live in.

Jezra   But at what cost, Mister President?

The President in deep thought.

President   Hmm?

Jezra   Surely the eradication of a complete civilisation is genocide?

President   We must all be willing to make sacrifice for the greater good of the majority, Jezra. It is a price we must pay for our freedom and integrity. I am willing to make that sacrifice and suffer the burden that comes with great responsibility. You must put any negative thoughts you may have aside and be focussed on the conflict ahead of us. Is that CLEAR?

Jezra   [*uncertainly*] Yes… Of course…

The President steps away from the table and views the image on the screen.

President   Very well then. Our meeting is concluded.

Exit others. The large screen now shows a clear image of Planet Earth in all its glory. The President resumes his seat, and smiles victoriously.

Suspenseful background music.

Lights fade.

Music fades.

SCENE NINE

Psychiatrist's office.

The Psychiatrist consults her notes.

Psychiatrist You said previously that you have felt alienated?

Old Man Now more than ever. I don't understand my place in the world like I used to. Something has changed. Something I have no control over.

Psychiatrist This latest dream certainly suggests that supposition. You evidently feel under attack by others outside of your influence. Would that be correct?

The Old Man nods.

Old Man It's a madness beyond comprehension. It's as though I've forfeited my identity.

The Psychiatrist considers at length.

Psychiatrist We're making progress.

The Psychiatrist makes notes.

Old Man Is that the *royal* we?

Psychiatrist [*looks up*] Hmm?

Old Man You're assuming that I am in accordance with your analytical perspective?

Psychiatrist It's all a matter of interpretation.

Old Man In what way?

Long pause.

Psychiatrist   Philosopher Friedrich Nietzsche believed that all dreams are works of fiction sparked by nervous stimuli. Each dream lends itself to the instinct that is prevalent in that moment. As you are an experienced writer, this is particularly true in your case.

Old Man   So you think that my brain is creating an ongoing storyline which, when interpreted, will make sense?

Psychiatrist   [*nods*] We're slowly unlocking the meaning behind your dreams. They are indicative of your… *condition*. You are on a journey of discovery, don't you see?

Old Man   I only see what is in my head. It stays with me. Controls me. [*Pause*] I'm not used to being a puppet. I don't understand who is pulling the strings, and for what purpose.

Psychiatrist   I assure you that nobody but yourself – your *inner* self – is pulling the strings. All aspects of your imaginings emanate from your own experience and thought process. For instance, in your dream, the President is an authoritarian, willing to commit genocide to achieve his ends.

Old Man   A formidable and dangerous presence.

Psychiatrist   I believe that he is representative of your nemesis.

The Old Man considers this contention.

Old Man   My nemesis…

Long pause.

Psychiatrist   He spoke of a new chapter.

Old Man   What of it?

Psychiatrist   Don't you see? This is clearly a metaphor. It's as if you are creating a work of art in your head.

The Old Man looks irritated.

Old Man   I'm creating *nothing*. It's not of my making. You don't get it. I'm beginning to think that you never will. [*Long pause*] I… I'm sorry. It's because I am so tired…

Psychiatrist   Dreams are subconscious. None of us can control them. They're part of our DNA, if you will. But they are subliminal in nature.

Old Man   Of course. You're right.

Long pause.

Psychiatrist   Tell me about your next dream…

Lights fade.

SCENE TEN

Suspenseful background music.

Darkly lit nondescript room. Square table, with three wooden chairs, centre stage. Large screen, upstage centre, showing night scene of forest with lit cabins in distance, through window.

Sitting around the table are three people: Habel, Santon and Jezra.

Music fades.

Habel So it's decided.

Jezra For the good of the people.

Santon looks nervous.

Santon I… I don't know… I still have some concerns, Habel.

Habel [*irritated*] We've gone over this a thousand times.

Santon I know… But the risks- [*Looks to others*] They're so great. When I

think of the consequences…

Jezra It has to be done. We have to be committed. It's all or nothing.

Santon But what if it fails?

Jezra It won't fail, Santon. We have to succeed. For the cause.

Habel Jezra's right. We have no other choice.

Jezra He wasn't elected by the people. He elected him*self*… him and his cronies.

It was a rigged election. The people had no say. How can that be right?

Habel stands, leans on table, and faces Santon.

Habel He's been lining his own pockets for years. How can he be the richest man

on the planet? It's obscene. He stuffs his face with caviar while the rest of

the population starve.

Jezra People are dying by the thousands because of his rule. Innocent people.

You must know that?

Santon [*sadly*] I know… But…

Poignant pause.

Habel   But what?

Santon   Who will replace him when he's… *gone*?

Habel paces the room.

Jezra   The Order will get the message: that the people can no longer tolerate corruption. A new Order. A new President. It can't be any worse than it is already.

Habel   A new beginning.

Jezra   Just think of the difference it would make to our world if he was no longer there to rule with impunity? People will be able to vote. A return to a democratically elected leader. A new beginning.

Santon   But what if they replace him with one of his cronies? We'll be back to square one. What then?

Habel   Then the struggle goes on. It's a chance we have to take.

Santon   Even so…

Jezra   We have to be fully committed.

Santon   Perhaps we should have a backup plan, in case-

Habel faces Santon.

Habel   [*angry*] We don't *need* a backup plan. We will succeed. We *have* to. We mustn't fill our thoughts with failure. There's too much at stake.

Jezra   When the Order was first created, after the last great conflict, it was a
noble institution. It served the people fairly and with compassion. With
this regime it has become a laughing stock throughout Mendetia. An
Order that seeks only to serve itself; it treats its people with contempt.

Habel   [*To Santon*] How many innocent family members have been lost because
of the President's policies?

Santon in deep contemplation.

Santon   Too many…

Jezra   Too many by far.

Habel resumes his seat.

Habel   My grandfather was taken by the authorities. It's such a cruel end to a
long life. So unjust. It makes me ashamed to work for the Order. [*Looks
to others*] We should *all* feel ashamed.

Jezra   The people are conditioned to accept the Order's rules. Afraid of the
consequences if they don't do as they are told.

Habel   [*to Santon*] Are you with us, Santon?

Santon   Under this President's regime they took my brother. He made a mistake…
and paid with his life. How can that be right? [*Looks to others*] I'm *with* you.

Long pause.

Habel   One day the pages of history will show that our actions were justified. That
there is such a thing as humanity in this mad existence; that people don't

have to succumb to the tyranny of an Order led by a lunatic. There is an alternative solution. [*Rises*] With strength of purpose and unity, we can change our world for the better. A new world. One fit to live in; with peace and harmony. For the greater good of the majority.

Habel places his hand upon the centre of the table. Jezra rises and solemnly places her hand upon Habel's.

Jezra   For the greater good of the majority.

Santon rises and solemnly places his hand upon Jezra's.

Santon   For the greater good of the majority.

They each look to each other with earnest expressions.

Suspenseful background music.

Lights fade.

Music fades.

End of Act One.

ACT TWO

SCENE ONE

Sad music.

Psychiatrist's office.

The Psychiatrist consults her notes.

Music fades.

Psychiatrist   Do you feel that order needs to be restored?

Old Man   Order has broken down. It no longer works... Not for me, anyway.

Psychiatrist   And it's worth fighting for?

The old Man looks pleadingly at the Psychiatrist.

Old Man   It's worth dying for.

Long pause.

Psychiatrist   Carl Jung was the founder of analytical psychology. Have you heard of him?

Old Man   Yes.

Psychiatrist   He suggests that the psyche in all of us is made up of three parts: Consciousness, personal unconsciousness and collective unconsciousness.

Old Man   Meaning?

The Psychiatrist consults her notes.

Psychiatrist   The psyche creates our realisation of self. Our identity. If we apply his theory to your… *situation*… perhaps we can unravel the meaning behind your dream. The ultimate goal for all of us is to achieve a fulfilled life. Do you see your life as unfulfilled?

Old Man   I no longer feel in control. So… yes.

Psychiatrist   In your dream the rebels were plotting the removal of the President of the World Governing Order?

Old Man   So it would seem.

Psychiatrist   And that innocent people have been lost because of the breakdown of
order?

Old Man   Through no fault of their own.

Psychiatrist   This may be a manifestation of your consciousness; that you see order as
disintegrating in your life. Your personal unconsciousness has created a
storyline in keeping with your creative ability as a writer. Your collective
unconsciousness sees the breakdown of order as a disruptive force that must
be resisted.

The Old Man looks defeated.

Old Man   I think I'm too tired to resist anything.

Psychiatrist   The brain is a powerful organ. It's said that we only use ten percent of its
potential. Dreams are created by experience and emotions.

The Old Man smiles feebly.

Old Man   My inner demons?

The Psychiatrist nods.

Psychiatrist   We all have them. It's part of the human condition. It's knowing what they
represent.

Old Man   The lunatics seem to be taking over the asylum.

Long pause.

Psychiatrist   Tell me about your next dream…

Lights fade.

SCENE TWO

Suspenseful background music.

A dimly-lit dungeon. Large screen, upstage centre, showing bricked wall with ominous pock-marked bullet holes.

> *Habel, Jezra and Santon, each bloodied, bruised, and blindfolded, are tied to fixed posts spread out in a line, centre stage. The President enters slowly, stage left, and paces to and fro behind his captives.*

Music fades.

President   Did you really think that your act of treachery would not be exposed for what it is? [*Smiles feebly*] You insult my intelligence. I have eyes and ears everywhere in Mendetia. Nothing of any note escapes my attention - especially when it concerns a plot to eradicate my very existence. I have prevented countless attempts on my life – more than you could ever know - and will continue to do so throughout my reign. My role as leader of the World Governing Order will endure until I am willing to relinquish power. I am the sole leader. I have ultimate control over life and death. Your lives, and the lives of all those that go against my rule, are meaningless to me.

Habel   One day the people will rise up against you.

President   The people are of no consequence. They will ultimately do as I say.

I have them in the palm of my hands. [*Accentuates*] I can crush them at any

time I choose.

Jezra   How can life be so meaningless to you?

President   It's a dog-eat-dog world, Jezra. The lives of others mean little in the

grand scheme of things. For the greater good of the majority. Surely even

you can see that?

Santon   But to destroy a whole civilisation? Innocent lives?

The President looks upon his captives with disdain.

President   You fools. Inhabitants of other worlds must be removed to accommodate

the people of Mendetia; otherwise… we perish. Our very existence, the

future of our kind, depends on resettlement in new lands. Our planet is

on its knees. Time is of the essence.

Habel   How did a sociopath like you ever get to be a leader of good people?

The President looks to Habel with intensity.

President   Through political persuasion and manipulation, Habel. The people elected

me many years ago, and I have ensured my continuing legacy by

eliminating my adversaries. The people insisted upon strong leadership in a

time of crisis... I have simply complied with their demands.

Santon   The people will see you for what you are. The *real* you: an authoritarian

and a coward.

The President is incensed.

President   Brave words for a condemned man, Santon. I am proud to be an authoritarian. But a coward? No. People like you and your kind will never understand how people like me are created. We wait in the shadows until it is the right moment to strike. And when that moment comes, we step into the light and make our declarations heard. The people are grateful for the courage and conviction shown. They can be controlled by fear and intimidation.

Jezra   It doesn't take courage to be a dictator.

President   I beg to differ. It takes courage to assume command in a time of upheaval. Strong leadership means making decisions that others may find… offensive.

Habel   To eliminate people just because of their age. How can you live with *that*?

President   You don't understand. Dwindling food supplies mean a need for a reduced population. It is a necessary sacrifice I am willing to make.

Habel   And when *you* are of a certain age?

The President considers at length.

President   I am immune to such considerations. [*Remorseful look in his eyes*] You have no notion of what it takes to be a great leader; it takes sacrifice… commitment. You think I've had it easy? When I was young, my mother left us. I was raised by my father. He was cold and calculating. He wasn't afflicted with affection of any kind. All that mattered was perception: *"Keep your chin up. Stop slouching. Don't let others see your weaknesses. You must be a killer in all transactions. Never admit defeat."* I've lived up to his ideals all my life. It hasn't been easy, but it's been a successful strategy…

Santon   It's turned you into a psychopath.

President   You see that as a weakness. I see it as a strength. The characteristics of a psychopath make for a perfect leader in times of crisis. I have a lack of remorse that people like you find distasteful, and I remain undaunted by a lack of etiquette and fair play. These are perfect attributes that allow a leader to flourish while others submit to failure.

Jezra   But at what cost?

President   It is a price worth paying. I am not hampered by the baggage of egalitarianism.

Santon   Destiny will see you for what you are.

President   My legacy is already assured. History will show that the survival of Mendetians meant sacrifice and self-determination; that the blood, sweat and tears, freely given, was for the greater good of the majority.

Habel   Let Jezra and Santon go.

Jezra   NO Habel. We're in this together.

Habel   It was all *my* making. I *made* them join me.

Santon   Jezra's right, Habel. It was a just cause.

President   A cause you are prepared to die for? [*Incidentally*] How touching…

Jezra   You wouldn't understand. Your kind never will.

President   On the contrary. We're more alike than you might realise. We're both committed to a cause we believe in, and we are willing to make the ultimate sacrifice to achieve our aims.

Habel   Get it over with. We all know how this ends.

President   All in good time.

Long pause.

Jezra   You're a sick man.

President   Is it any wonder? Yes, I'm sick. Sick of those who are disloyal to me and to the World Governing Order. You each swore your allegiance, and you betrayed that oath.

Santon   You left us no choice.

President   You should have chosen the correct path. You could have been instrumental in the creation of a new world. A world we can be proud of. A new Mendetia. Think of it… [*Looks heavenwards as if in a trance*] My legacy will be assured. People will treat me as if I was a god. I will have absolute power in this new realm…

Habel   Nobody can ever have absolute power. Not even you…

The President looks to his captives at length.

President   I disagree.

Suspenseful background music.

The President looks to stage left, nods, and exits stage right. Three armed guards enter, stage left; they each stand beside Habel, Jezra and Santon, and raise their weapons to the side of their heads.

Lights fade until pitch black.

Three loud gunshots are heard…

Music fades.

SCENE THREE

Psychiatrist's office.

The Psychiatrist consults her notes.

Psychiatrist It's evident to me that you see the President as indicative of your troubles. He perhaps represents a negative force against which you feel powerless. Would that be a correct assumption?

The Old Man nods.

Old Man It seems plausible. But why?

Psychiatrist All dreams are subjective and open to interpretation. It's only through analysis and discourse that we can establish their full meaning. [*Long pause*] What is your darkest fear at this moment?

Old Man That I am losing my mind.

Psychiatrist And why do you think that is?

Old Man Forces beyond my control.

Psychiatrist   And that troubles you…

The Old Man looks visibly shaken.

Old Man   It terrifies me. You see, I've always *been* in control. Can you imagine what it's like to live in a world that no longer makes sense?

Psychiatrist   I imagine it must seem very strange, but-

Old Man   STRANGE? I'm living in a nightmarish fantasy, and yet it all seems so real. I'm no longer in charge of my destiny. I've lost my way. I need to find myself again. Before it's too late. It feels as though I'm slipping away into oblivion. [*Long pause*] I feel so… lost.

The Psychiatrist looks to the Old Man with some concern.

Psychiatrist   I believe we are much closer to the truth.

Old Man   The truth?

Psychiatrist   These dreams you have been experiencing are a representation of your innermost fears. You feel helpless against a negative force represented by the President who is an authoritarian. A dictator. The rebels were executed as a punishment for going against his rule. The rebels represent your internal struggle.

The Old Man looks lost in his thoughts.

Old Man   It feels like a losing battle.

Long pause.

Intruder   Tell me about your next dream.

Lights fade.

SCENE FOUR

Suspenseful background music.

The President's office. Dimly lit. Impressive desk. Large screen showing elaborate emblem of World Governing Order.

> *Sat at the desk is the President, reading information from a screen. A young man (Intruder) enters stage left. The President looks up at his Visitor, with vague disinterest.*

Music fades.

President   Ah… You asked to see me?

Visitor   Yes Mister President.

> *The President rises and approaches the young man.*

President   I've heard good things about your work in the field of transtemporal displacement. Your input is invaluable to the World Governing Order. Without your department's work we would be unable to gauge our efforts of resettlement.

Visitor   I have major concerns, Mister President.

President   Oh?

Visitor   I've learned that our conquest is not without drastic consequence. Mass destruction of cities throughout the new world.

The President moves away from the Visitor and views the large screen which now shows the new planet amongst the stars.

President   An inevitable outcome. A sacrifice of the highest order. Many will die in the pursuit of a new tomorrow. [*Glances briefly at Visitor*] It cannot be avoided. We must be strong. Vigilant. Your work has shown the outcome of our plans. War is essential. Through chaos and destruction comes a new life. A new beginning for the citizens of Mendetia. A lasting legacy. [*Smiles faintly*] Your service will not go unrecognised... or unrewarded. Your future is assured.

The Visitor looks forlorn.

Visitor   [*distantly*] It's my future that *worries* me.

President   You cannot change the future. What concerns do you have?

Visitor   Guilt.

President   Guilt?

The Visitor nods in sad resignation.

Visitor   A lifetime of it.

The President looks agitated.

President   May I remind you that it is unlawful for anyone working in your department to abuse one's position for personal reasons. It is a punishable offence. You risk becoming an Undesirable. You *know* what happens to Undesirables?

The Visitor looks down in resignation.

Visitor   Death…

The President nods solemnly in agreement.

President   Because you have been so useful to the Order in our military operations, I

am willing to overlook your… misdemeanour… [*As an afterthought*] *For*

now…

Visitor   [*deadpan*] Thank you Mister President.

The President now has his back to the Visitor and looks once more at

the large screen which shows the new planet in more detail. The Visitor

takes out a dagger from his inside pocket and conceals it behind his back.

President   Is that all?

Visitor   [*solemnly*] Not quite.

President   Come and look at our new domain. A new beginning. [*The Visitor stands*

slightly behind the President and looks at the new planet] Isn't it

magnificent?

The President glances momentarily at the Visitor.

Visitor   [*sadly*] Yes... It is.

President   They said it would be impossible to find a planet worthy of resettlement;

that our future is to remain on this godforsaken dying planet until its

last embers. And yet here we are: on the cusp of a new dawn. A chance

for future generations to survive and flourish. Millions will die as in all

wars, but through aggression comes triumph; through adversity comes

prosperity. [*The Visitor now stands directly behind the President – he slowly retrieves his dagger with his right hand, and stands ready*] Our

destiny is in our hands.

Visitor   On that we agree.

The Visitor clasps his left hand firmly over the President's mouth; with

his right hand he calmly slits the President's throat.

Powerful background music.

The President collapses to the ground, dead. Visitor exits stage left.

Lights fade.

Music fades.

SCENE FIVE

Psychiatrist's office.

The Psychiatrist consults her notes.

Psychiatrist   It seems that your younger self took matters into his own hands.

Old Man   A noble but futile gesture, it would seem...

Psychiatrist   Don't you feel a sense of justice from his actions?

The Old Man shakes his head.

Old Man   I'm not sure what I feel anymore...

Psychiatrist   It's natural to be ambivalent. It's only through self-analysis and introspection

that we are able to determine meanings behind our imaginings.

Old Man   You think I'm delusional?...

Psychiatrist   I think you're… troubled.

The Old Man looks blankly ahead.

Old Man   Troubled…

After deep thought the Psychiatrist has a revelation.

Psychiatrist   Have you heard of hypnotherapy?

Old Man   Yes.

Psychiatrist   You once called me your conscience.

Old Man   My Jiminy Cricket.

The Psychiatrist smiles faintly.

Psychiatrist   Then we share a bond. We have a valid connection. Do you agree?

Old Man   I agree.

Psychiatrist   Hypnotherapy works by tapping into your subconscious. Through

hypnosis and auto suggestion it is possible to open and validate meanings

behind your thought process. We gain entry into the dark recess of your

mind. We can open the door that has so far remained locked. Are you

willing and able to comply?

Old Man   Yes.

Psychiatrist   You *do* trust me?

Old Man   I do.

Psychiatrist   Then close your eyes.

Old Man   But I'm afraid I might not wake up.

Psychiatrist   You will wake up I assure you. [*The Old Man closes his eyes*] Can you hear me?

Old Man   I can hear you.

Psychiatrist   You are gently falling in the darkness. Your body feels as light as a feather. You cannot see anything except the darkness. You feel a cool breeze as you slowly descend to a place somewhere in the far reaches of your past. I will count down from ten, and when I reach one you will open your eyes. Let your mind see the characters in your dreams. Who they *really* are.

Lights fade.

Haunting music.

A pale blue light now on the Old Man and the Psychiatrist.

Psychiatrist (cont'd) Ten… nine… eight… seven… six… five… four… three… two… one…

The Old Man opens his eyes, leans back in his chair, and surveys the scene.

SCENE SIX

Ten characters, dressed in black, emerge from stage left and right: #1 (Santon), #2 (Jezra), #3 (Patora), #4 (Habel), #5 (Delgin), #6 (Hetta), #7 (Samile), #8 (Fedo), #9 (Grogan), #10 (President); they form a semicircle centre stage before the Old Man. Large screen shows pale moonlit sky.

#8 steps forward and sits opposite the Old Man who is confused and unsure of his surroundings. The Psychiatrist continues to stand, observing the proceedings.

#8 (Fedo)   Hello grandad. How are you? You are looking well. My probation officer finally came through. [*The Old Man looks puzzled, as he does throughout*] I've got a job at long last. Hopefully it will keep me on the straight and narrow. Life isn't easy, is it? I suppose it never has been really.

Old Man   [*to Psychiatrist*] There must be some mistake? He was a thief. An undesirable.

Psychiatrist   There's no mistake.

#8 looks to others with pity in his eyes, and shakes his head; he returns to his position in the group. #7 steps forward and sits opposite the Old Man.

#7 (Samile)   Sorry I haven't been in to see you lately dad. [*Gently strokes the Old Man's hair*] I've wanted to but I've been busy what with one thing and another. Divorce is so painful. Losing custody hurts so much. But enough about me. Are you well? Are they looking after you okay?

Old Man   [*to Psychiatrist*] But I don't recognise this person other than as a captive.

Psychiatrist   They were all part of your life.

#7 looks to others with pity in her eyes, and shakes her head; she returns to her position in the group. #1 steps forward and sits opposite the Old Man.

#1 (Santon) How's my favourite uncle? I now have a job at long last. I work as an assistant librarian at the local library. The pay's not great but it keeps me out of mischief. I became a proud union member because our jobs are at risk. They're making cutbacks but we'll fight it as best we can.

Old Man [*to Psychiatrist*] I don't understand. These people can't be real? He was a captured rebel.

Psychiatrist They are all *very* real. You conceived a storyline.

#1 looks to others with pity in his eyes, and shakes his head; he returns to his position in the group. #5 steps forward and sits opposite the Old Man.

#5 (Delgin) I always looked up to you as you were my older, wiser, brother. I remember how you stood up for me when I was bullied at school. You gave that boy a black eye. He never bullied me again. You taught me to stick up for myself and not be intimidated by anyone.

Old Man [*to Psychiatrist*] I had a brother? But he worked for the World Governing Order.

Psychiatrist [*shakes head*] He is your brother.

#5 looks to others with pity in his eyes, and shakes his head; he returns to his position in the group. #2 steps forward and sits opposite the Old Man.

#2 (Jezra) It's good to see you again, grandad. I'm sorry you haven't been yourself lately. I hope they've been looking after you okay? I've got some good news for you: you're going to be a great grandad. Isn't that something? I was always a rebel when I was young, but now I feel very grown up.

Old Man [*to Psychiatrist*] A great grandad… But she was executed?

Psychiatrist Only in your imagination.

#2 looks to others with pity in her eyes, and shakes her head; she returns to her position in the group. #4 steps forward and sits opposite the Old Man.

#4 (Habel) I hope you are feeling okay grandad? You look well, all things considered. As shop steward at the hospital, I'm calling on all members to strike for better pay. Hopefully they'll see sense and do the right thing. You always taught me to fight for what I believed in. I'll always be grateful to you for that.

Old Man [*to Psychiatrist*] This is difficult for me to take in. He was the lead rebel.

Psychiatrist A character you created.

#4 looks to others with pity in his eyes, and shakes his head; he returns to his position in the group. #3 steps forward and sits opposite the Old Man.

#3 (Patora) I will always cherish the memory of our childhood. As my big brother you will never know how much I looked up to you. Oh, we had our ups and downs, but I always loved you and still do. You always taught me not to be a sheep, and lead from the front, but I have never had your confidence. I'm very proud of you and always will be.

Old Man [*to Psychiatrist*] My sister… But she worked for the Order.

Psychiatrist She will always be your sister.

#3 looks to others with pity in her eyes, and shakes her head; she returns to her position in the group. #9 steps forward and sits opposite the Old Man.

#9 (Grogan)   I'm so proud that you're my father. I will always look up to you no matter what. We haven't always got on but I appreciate all that you did for me. I never really showed any gratitude. But thank you. I'll soon be joining a demonstration against the faceless bureaucrats that tell us how to live our lives. You've always shown great strength of purpose. The only time I've seen you cry is when my sister died in that terrible car crash all those years ago. I still miss her.

The Old Man looks to the Psychiatrist with a flicker of recognition.

Old Man   A car crash…

#9 looks to others with pity in his eyes, and shakes his head; he returns to his position in the group. #6 steps forward and sits opposite the Old Man.

#6 (Hetta)   It's me. Your wife. We've been married now for over fifty years. When we were first married we were very poor. We didn't have two pennies to rub together, but we made do. It's what you did in those days. We loved each very much and had a good life together. I've not been so well lately. The doctor tells me that my breathing is very weak. It's one of the joys of getting old, I suppose. I will always love you no matter what.

Old Man   My wife…

Psychiatrist   You had a life. A family that cared.

#6 looks to others with pity in her eyes, and shakes her head; she returns to her position in the group. #10 steps forward and sits opposite the Old Man.

#10 (President) As your healthcare practitioner I have to be brutally honest with you. Although you are in relatively good physical health for your age, your cognitive abilities have diminished over the last few months. I'm afraid you are in the advanced stage of mental decline. This will seem strange to you. Even a little frightening. But we'll make you as comfortable as we can.

Old Man   [*to Psychiatrist*] I never liked that doctor.

Psychiatrist   He was there to help you.

#10 looks to others with pity in his eyes, and shakes his head; he returns to his position in the group. The group slowly exits stage left and right.

Psychiatrist (cont'd) Close your eyes. [*The Old Man closes his eyes*] I will count down from ten. When I reach one you will open your eyes. You will remember everything. Ten… nine… eight… seven… six… five… four… three… two… one…

Lights fade.

Music fades.

SCENE SEVEN

Psychiatrist's office.

The Old Man gradually opens his eyes.

Old Man   That was quite a spell you cast over me.

Psychiatrist   It came from within yourself. I am merely the conduit.

The Old Man looks confused.

Old Man   All those people…

Psychiatrist They each had a part to play.

Old Man   How did you know?

Psychiatrist I didn't. *You* did.

Old Man   Were they all who they said they were?

Psychiatrist Oh yes. Part of your history.

Old Man   My history… I was beginning to think I no longer *had* a history. It felt like
I no longer belonged.

Psychiatrist As though you were from another planet.

Old Man   Mendetia…

Psychiatrist Your mind has been working hard all this time trying to make sense of
a world now changed beyond recognition.

Old Man   What is to become of me?

Psychiatrist You have a life to live regardless of your circumstances.

Old Man   It's all so…

A long silence ensues.

Psychiatrist Frustrating?

The Old Man nods.

Old Man   Yes.

Psychiatrist   It comes with the territory, I'm afraid.

Poignant pause. The Old Man looks to the Psychiatrist with sadness in his eyes.

Old Man   You're not real, are you…

The Psychiatrist smiles slightly.

Psychiatrist   I'm as real as you think I am.

Old Man   Who are you?

Brief vision of a terrible car crash shown on the large screen.

Psychiatrist   Someone you once knew.

Old Man   I do feel an affinity with you. Were we close?

Brief vision of a terrible car crash shown on the large screen.

Psychiatrist   Oh yes… We were very close. Once upon a time.

Old Man   I have such a slender grip on reality.

Psychiatrist   You've created your own internal reality. As a means of escape...

Old Man   What am I escaping from?

The Psychiatrist looks to the Old Man with tears in her eyes.

Psychiatrist   From yourself...

Lights fade.

Sad music.

SCENE EIGHT

A kitchen. Large screen shows a garden full of colour through a back door.

> *The Old Man is at the sink washing dishes; his wife (Hetta) is beside him busily drying the wet dishes. They are happy in each other's company.*

Music fades.

Wife   I bought a bottle of red wine for later.

Old Man   Sounds good. What's the occasion?

> *The wife looks to her husband with some concern.*

Wife   Our anniversary of course.

> *The Old Man looks confused.*

Old Man   Really?

Wife   You've been quite forgetful lately.

> *The Old Man looks sheepish.*

Old Man   Men are not very good at remembering dates. Especially anniversaries. [*Pause*] Sorry.

Wife   You've never forgotten before?

Old Man   Getting old.

Wife   Forty-nine years.

Old Man   Hmm?

Wife   We've been married for forty-nine years.

The Old Man looks confused.

Old Man   Really? How is that possible?

Wife   [*smiles*] I sometimes wonder…

Old Man   I didn't know we were that bloody old.

Wife   We're no longer spring chickens, that's for sure.

Old Man   I can't keep track of time. It seems only five minutes ago when we were first married. In the blink of an eye our children have grown up and left the nest.

Wife   That's life, I'm afraid.

Old Man   I look in the mirror these days and I don't recognise that old fart looking back at me.

Wife   I'm worried about you.

Old Man   Why?

Wife   You've not been yourself lately.

Old Man   What do you mean?

Wife   Oh, I don't know… Lots of little things, I suppose.

Old Man   Like what?

Wife   You forget where you put your house keys quite often.

Old Man   They seem to have a life of their own these days. I swear they get up and walk away. [*Considers at length*] Same with the remote.

Wife   I've noticed you seem a bit preoccupied. Are you feeling alright?

Old Man   [*dismissively*] I'm fine. Don't fuss.

Wife   I'm worried.

Old Man   Don't be.

Wife   Even so…

The Old Man stops washing dishes and turns to his wife.

Old Man   [*irate*] I *told* you. I'm fine. How many times do I have to fucking *tell* you? [*Contrite. Long pause*] I'm sorry. I'm… I'm so sorry.

The Old Man and his wife look to each other as though for the first time.

Sad music.

Lights fade.

SCENE NINE

A wooden bench in a lonely dark street. Large screen shows an old street lamp amongst the trees, casting its pale light below.

The Old Man, wearing an old coat, sits on the bench, looking lost in his thoughts. After a long while the Old Man is approached stage left by his Daughter (Samile).

Music fades.

Daughter   Hello dad. We've been out looking for you.

The Old Man looks up in some confusion.

Old Man   Have you?

Daughter   We were worried. Wondered where you were.

Old Man   I went for a walk. Thought it might clear my head. There seems to be a
lot of cobwebs lately.

The Daughter sits next to her father.

Daughter   You didn't let mum know where you were going.

Old Man   Didn't I?

Daughter   She was worried about you. We all were.

Old Man   I started walking until it got dark. Then I seem to have lost my bearings.

Daughter   You haven't been yourself lately.

The old Man looks intently at his Daughter.

Old Man   If I'm not myself… who *am* I? All my life I knew what it meant to be me. I
had a part to play. A sense of purpose. But now… Things are not as clear
to me as they once were. They've become… foggy. It feels like I'm swimming
against the tide.

Daughter   I know it must be hard for you.

Old Man   I must have been a salmon in my last life.

The Daughter smiles.

Daughter   At least you haven't lost your sense of humour.

Old Man   It's losing my sense of purpose that worries me.

Daughter   In what way?

Old Man   Parts of my life are already just a blur. How long will it be before I forget who I am? What will be my legacy when all is said and done?

Daughter   [*gently*] You'll always be my dad. No matter what.

The Old Man looks to his daughter tenderly.

Old Man   Of course.

Long pause. The Daughter looks to the heavens.

Daughter   Think it might rain.

Old Man   Maybe it will help clear my head.

Daughter   We all lose ourselves in our thoughts sometimes dad.

Old Man   You sound like your sister.

The Daughter looks pensive.

Daughter   It's been nearly ten years…

Old Man   Hmm?

Daughter   Since the accident. I still can't believe she's… gone.

Cold reality dawns on the Old Man.

Old Man   The accident…

Daughter   It's a day I'll never forget.

The Old Man looks ahead as if in another world.

Old Man   [*to himself*] I wish I could say the same...

Sad music.

Lights fade.

SCENE TEN

Doctor's consulting room. Large screen shows hospital complex through window.

Sat at a desk is a Doctor (President); across from him is the Old Man and his Wife (Hetta). The Doctor reviews various notes in front of him.

Music fades.

Doctor   [*to the Old Man*] I've reviewed the results of your test.

Wife   What is your opinion, Doctor?

The Doctor looks concerned.

Doctor   I'm afraid it shows a marked decline in cognitive ability. [*To the Old Man*] We'll conduct further tests such as a brain CT scan to determine the root cause of your condition. Meanwhile we'll put you on medication that will relieve some of the symptoms and make you more comfortable.

Old Man   Am I losing my marbles, Doctor?

Long pause.

| **Doctor** | Your memory function isn't working as well as it should. It's progressive but with the right medication we should be able to slow down the process over time. You will experience reduced semantic memory which inhibits communication and understanding of everyday objects. [*To Hetta*] We'll arrange a nurse to visit your husband on a regular basis to provide support and administer the necessary drugs. |

The Old Man's Wife wipes a tear away with a tissue.

| **Wife** | It seems such a cruel injustice. It's not fair. |

| **Doctor** | I'm afraid so. |

| **Wife** | What can I expect, Doctor? How will I cope? |

| **Doctor** | There will be good and bad days. Some days your husband will seem distant, distracted. Perhaps internalised. As though… |

| **Old Man** | From another planet... |

Long pause.

| **Doctor** | [*to the Old Man*] Is there anything you'd like to ask me? Anything at all. |

The Old Man considers at length.

| **Old Man** | Do you know what happens to a star when it dies? |

Long pause.

| **Doctor** | I'm… I'm not sure I understand? |

The Old Man smiles to himself.

Old Man   It becomes a black hole. [*The Doctor and the Old Man's wife look blankly*

at him. Long pause] Metaphor…

Sad music.

Lights fade.

SCENE ELEVEN

Care home. Dimly lit small room. A bed is against the side wall. Large screen shows pale

moonlight through horizontal window blinds.

> *The Old Man sits alone in an armchair staring blankly ahead. After a long*
>
> *time a uniformed Nurse (Intruder) enters stage left; he is carrying a small*
>
> *tray that has various pills upon it.*

Music fades.

Nurse   I've brought you your medication.

Old Man   Where am I?

> *The Nurse puts the tray down upon a small table, and stands beside the*
>
> *Old Man.*

Nurse   South Newman Residential Care Home. You've been here since your wife

passed away. Don't you remember?

> *The Old Man is in deep thought.*

Old Man   My wife?

Nurse   She was a lovely lady. You sold the family home and moved in here.

Old Man   Really?

Nurse   Déjà vu.

Old Man   What?

Nurse   Déjà vu. I think we may have had this conversation before. [*To himself*] Now and then…

Old Man   Am I boring you?

Nurse   Of course not. Here. [*The Nurse hands a pill in a small paper cup*] Take your pill.

The Old Man does as he is told and puts the pill in his mouth followed by a gulp of water from another paper cup. The Nurse hands him two more in succession and he does the same.

Old Man   It's a wonder I don't rattle what with all these pills you keep giving me.

Nurse   Doctor's orders I'm afraid.

Old Man   Doctors… Where would we be without doctors?

The Nurse smiles ironically.

Nurse   Dead probably.

Old Man   Well that's a happy thought, I must say.

Nurse   At least you haven't lost your sense of humour.

Old Man   I seem to have lost everything else.

Nurse   Now now.

Old Man   I think I'm a lost cause.

Nurse   Nobody is a lost cause.

Old Man   That's very diplomatic of you.

Nurse   You've lived a life. More than you could possibly know.

Old Man   You seem to know more about me than I know myself.

Nurse   Your mind has erased a lot of your experiences. It's part of your condition I'm afraid.

Old Man   So I'm told.

Nurse   It's sadly all too common. [*Poignant pause*] Too cruel.

Old Man   Sometimes I can remember things from my past. But it's often jumbled. They tell me I was a writer.

Nurse   Yes… You were.

Old Man   And that I have a family.

Nurse   Who care about you very much.

Old Man   I can't remember them but I'm sure they're very kind.

Nurse   Yes. They are.

Old Man   Tell me… Have we met before?

Nurse   I've been your carer for many years now. So… yes.

The Old Man sees the Nurse's tattoo on his forearm.

Old Man   I've noticed that we share the same tattoo. That's quite a coincidence.

The Nurse looks sad.

Nurse   Yes… I suppose it is.

Long pause.

Old Man   I suppose you'll be off to pastures new before long like all the others?

Nurse   Oh no. No… I'm here for the long run. You can't get rid of me that easily.

Old Man   I don't know why but I'm very glad to hear that.

Nurse   I'm glad too.

Long pause.

Old Man   What is your name?

Nurse   John.

Old Man   I'll probably ask you again later.

The Nurse leans over the Old Man and briefly puts his hand upon the Old Man's shoulder.

Nurse   You can ask me as many times as you like.

Old Man   You're very understanding.

The Nurse stands.

Nurse   It comes with the job. Is there anything I can get for you?

The Old Man thinks long and hard.

Old Man   I'd like to read the newspaper but I seem to have misplaced my glasses.

Nurse   I'll see if I can find them for you.

The Nurse scours the room looking for the Old Man's glasses.

Old Man   That's very kind of you. They can't be far. I'd lose my head if it wasn't screwed on.

The Nurse looks through a set of drawers.

Nurse   You must have been a magpie in your last life. I've never seen so many things packed into a drawer, I must say.

Old Man   I don't like to throw things away.

The Nurse finds the glasses.

Nurse   Here they are. [*The Nurse makes another surprising discovery*] Hello… What's this? [*He looks at a manuscript and then holds it up for the Old Man to see*] The Lost Galaxy by John Richard King.

Old Man   Is that my name?

Nurse   Yes.

The Old Man looks visibly moved. Long pause.

Old Man   Well… I'll be.

Emotional music.

Lights fade.

Music fades.

Play ends.

Playwright: **Colin Fantham** BA (hons)

Colin Fantham was born in Stratford-upon-Avon in 1957.
Having spent over 40 years in the insurance industry he
is now retired and devotes most of his energy to his
writing. Creative from an early age, Colin has written
several pieces of music and numerous scripts for stage
and screen.

Some examples of his work:

Henry's Last Act ©. A half hour original comedy series for
television. It is set in The Sunny Retreat retirement home
for entertainers. This gentle comedy centres around the
friendship between residents Henry, Edgar and Twinky, as
well as an abundance of other quirky characters, including
Jessica who is a teenage work-experience employee. Eight
episodes. PublishNation in Amazon.

The Folly (A Moment in Time) ©. A 5 act stage play. A late
Victorian period drama involving 2 families (The Hathertons
and the Buckleys) who happen to meet by a folly. Their
chance encounter leads to a path of destruction, love, but
ultimately self-enlightenment. Is the enchanted area of the
folly a reality, or from the mind of a man on the brink of
despair? Atmospheric and magical. PublishNation in Amazon.

Visitors from a Lost World ©. A 2 act stage play. Arthur, who
is an elderly gentleman, lives alone in a remote tower block
in London with only his fish Merlin for company. He
narrates his past to Merlin, and we see him in his youth
when he served his national service in the 1950s and fell in
love with Dotty. Funny, sad, and poignant. PublishNation in
Amazon.

The Final Chapter of A Strange Affair ©. A 2 act stage play. In 1969, Peter is a writer on the edge of madness. Suffering from writer's block, he is unable to meet the deadline for submission of his latest novel A Strange Affair. All is not as it seems, as Peter is troubled by the death of his wife Angela, who disappeared in mysterious circumstances. A chilling insight into the mind of a writer who is haunted by events of the past. And then there's George… Dark and frightening. PublishNation in Amazon.

A compilation of three plays: The Folly (A Moment In Time); Visitors from a Lost World; The Final Chapter of A Strange Affair. PublishNation in Amazon.

A film script based on the play Visitors from a Lost World. PublishNation in Amazon.

Colin Fantham is a member of WriteOn script workshop in Cambridge, Writers Guild of GB, and a member of Geoffrey Whitworth Theatre.

For any and all enquiries: cjfantham57@sky.com